Mar

D1162341

DOGS SET III

Chihuahuas

Bob Temple
ABDO Publishing Company

visit us at
www.abdopub.com

Published by ABDO Publishing Company, 4940 Viking Drive, Suite 622, Edina, Minnesota 55435.

Printed in the United States.

Edited by: Paul Joseph

Photo credits: Peter Arnold, Inc.; Ron Kimball Photography

Library of Congress Cataloging-in-Publication Data

Temple, Bob.
     Chihuahuas / Bob Temple
          p. cm. — (Dogs. Set III)
      ISBN 1-57765-419-6
       1. Chihuahua (Dog breed)—Juvenile literature. [1. Chihuahua (Dog breed). 2. Dogs. 3. Pets] I. Title.

SF429.C45 T45 2000
636.76—dc21
                  00-036189

Contents

Where Dogs Come From

Dogs and people have been friends for a long time. Millions of people have dogs as family pets. Yet there was a time when dogs and humans did not live together. In fact, even today there are many members of the family that dogs come from that live in the wild.

Dogs are often called "canines." This is because they are from the species called Canidae, from the Latin word canis, which means "dog."

Besides the many **breeds** of dog that we have as pets, other members of this family of animals are wolves, foxes, and other wild dogs. They may not look like they come from the same family as a Chihuahua, but they do!

The Chihuahua comes from the same family as the wolf and fox.

Chihuahuas

Chihuahuas are from the "toy" group of dogs. In fact, they are the tiniest dog **breed**, weighing between two and four pounds (0.9 to 1.8 kg).

The Chihuahua got its name because the modern breed was discovered in 1850, in Chihuahua, Mexico.

Chihuahuas are popular dogs in America, but have become even more popular since the little Chihuahua began appearing in television commercials!

Opposite page: The Chihuahua is so small that even full-grown it can fit into your pocket or jacket.

What They're Like

Chihuahuas are happy, friendly little dogs that love to bounce around about as much as they like to rest in their owner's lap. Their bright eyes and large, pointed ears make them look alert and ready for action. And they are.

They are very smart and they learn very quickly. They love to be with their owners and other Chihuahuas, but they are shy around other **breeds** of dogs. They also are nervous around strangers. When they are nervous, they will stay close to their owners at all times.

Chihuahuas can be taken outside for short walks, but they need to live indoors. Because they are so small, they are perfect for people who live in an apartment or don't have a large yard.

Chihuahuas stay alert by using its pointed ears.

Coat and Color

Chihuahuas can have one of two different kinds of **coats**. Some Chihuahuas have a smooth coat, which is short and soft and looks glossy.

Other Chihuahuas have a long coat, which is very soft and can be flat or a little curly. Long-coated Chihuahuas also have a fringe of fur around their heads and feathered fur on their legs.

Chihuahuas can be a number of different colors, from sandy white to blue or even black. Many Chihuahuas are white and tan. Their eyes are usually dark, but some light-colored Chihuahuas have lighter eyes.

Opposite page: The long-coated Chihuahua has a fringe of fur around the head and legs.

Size

Chihuahuas are tiny little dogs. They usually weigh between two and four pounds (0.9 to 1.8 kg). They stand only about five inches tall (12.7 cm).

They have an apple-shaped skull and the very top might have a soft spot that never closes. The back is usually a little longer than the dog's height. The tail curves up over the back of the dog in a gentle arc.

Opposite page: The Chihuahua is one of the smallest breeds of dogs.

Care

Because they are so small, Chihuahuas don't need to be taken on long walks to get their exercise. Instead, playing with your dog inside your home or apartment is usually enough to keep them healthy. And your Chihuahua will love the attention. Chihuahuas should not be left outside in weather that is very hot or cold.

Even though they are small, Chihuahuas do need a lot of care. They need their ears cleaned regularly, up to once a week. Their teeth should be brushed weekly, too. Their nails need regular care to keep them from getting too long. Your Chihuahua is also going to need to have its **coat** brushed twice a week, even if it has the shorter, smooth coat.

All dogs need to get shots from the **veterinarian** every year. These shots help keep them from getting diseases like **distemper**. Most of all, your Chihuahua needs to be loved by the members of your family.

Chihuahuas need a lot of love and attention.

Feeding

All dogs need a proper **diet** to be a happy, healthy member of your family. Without good **nutrition**, your Chihuahua can get sick.

When you first buy your Chihuahua puppy, you should find out what kind of food the breeder was feeding it. You should continue to feed your dog the same food for a while. If you decide to change foods, you should do so gradually. This will keep the dog from getting an upset stomach.

Your **veterinarian** can help you decide what is the best food for your Chihuahua. Once you settle on a type of food, you shouldn't change it. Dogs don't like to have their diet changed very often. And make sure not to feed your dog leftovers from the

food you eat. Dogs were not meant to eat the same food as humans. You should always make sure your dog has plenty of clean, fresh water to drink.

All dogs need to be on a proper diet.

Things They Need

One of the reasons that Chihuahuas make great pets is that they don't need very much from their owners. They are the perfect dog for busy people, because they don't need long walks every day. A Chihuahua needs a nice, quiet place to rest. Your lap will be one of their favorite places.

Chihuahuas need to live indoors, and they don't need a whole lot of space. They can live in a small apartment in the middle of the city. They need a few toys to play with, like a small ball or a rope to tug on.

All dogs should have a collar with an identification tag that includes the owner's name, address, and telephone number. This will make it

easy for someone to contact you if your Chihuahua were to get lost. In some cities, dogs also need a **license**. And most dogs wear a tag that says they have gotten their rabies shot.

The Chihuahua needs a nice, quiet place to rest.

Puppies

Usually, Chihuahuas have a very small **litter** of about one to four puppies. If you find out that your Chihuahua is **pregnant,** you should provide a strong, warm box. This is where your dog will have its puppies. The puppies will need warmth, so you can put a heating pad covered by a towel or blanket into the box.

Dogs are **mammals**. This means they drink milk from their mother's body when they are first born. Like most small dogs, Chihuahua puppies grow very quickly. After just a few weeks, you can begin to feed them soft puppy food.

Because Chihuahuas are so small, they are very fragile. Their bones can break very easily, so you should be very careful when you hold the puppies. They should also be kept away from small children.

Glossary

breed: a group of dogs that share the same appearance and characteristics.

coat: the hair that covers a dog's body.

diet: the food that your dog eats.

distemper: a contagious disease that dogs sometimes get. It is caused by a virus.

license (LIE-sense): a tag worn by a dog indicating it has been registered with a city.

litter: the group of puppies a dog has in one pregnancy.

mammal: warm-blooded animals that feed their babies milk from the mother's body.

nutrition (new-TRISH-un): proper food and diet; nourishment.

pregnant: with one or more babies growing within the body.

veterinarian (VET-er-in-AIR-ian): an animal doctor; also called a vet.

Internet Sites

Chihuahua

http:///www.agilityability.com/

This site offers information on the Chihuahua and their agility ability. Included is information about the history of Chihuahuas, and their character. There are pictures of Chihuahuas and more.

The American Kennel Club Web Page

http://www.akc.org

Information about many breeds, including the Chihuahua. This page includes physical characteristics and a great deal about its history. You can also find breeder information. There is a message board for Chihuahua owners to exchange information.

Index